DRIVE

Nathan Clement

Front Street
Asheville, North Carolina

Copyright © 2008 by Nathan Clement
All rights reserved
Printed in China
Designed by Helen Robinson
First edition

CIP data is available

Front Street
An Imprint of Boyds Mills Press, Inc.
815 Church Street
Honesdale, Pennsylvania 18431

BUZZ z z

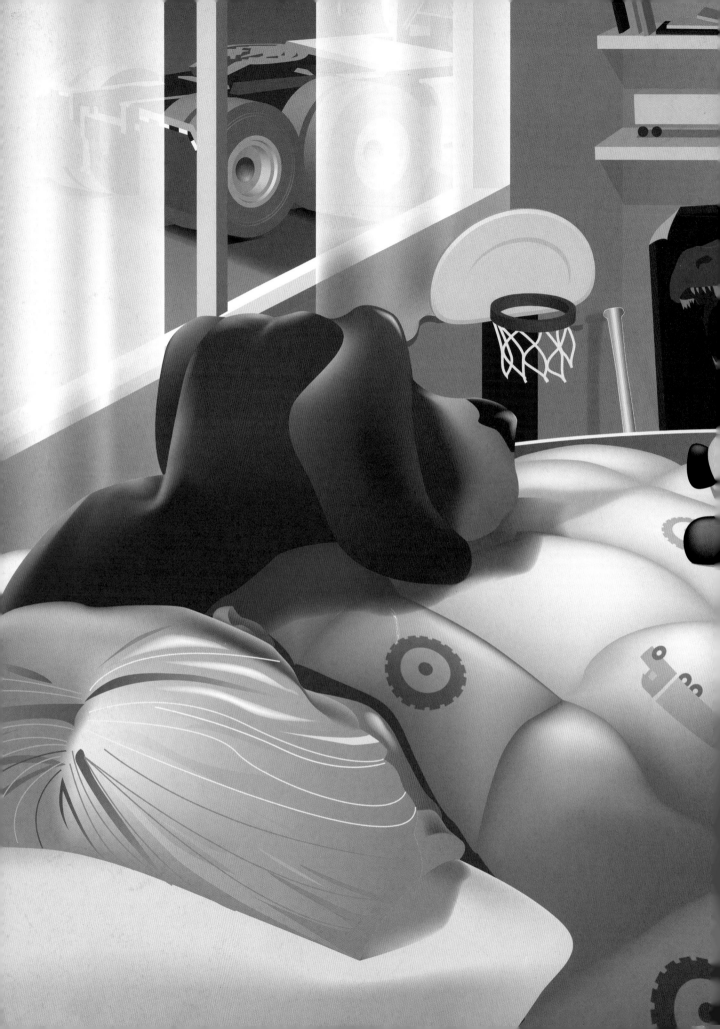

Daddy leaves
before
I wake up.

Daddy drives to work.

When his trailer is full,

he's ready to drive.

Daddy stays busy

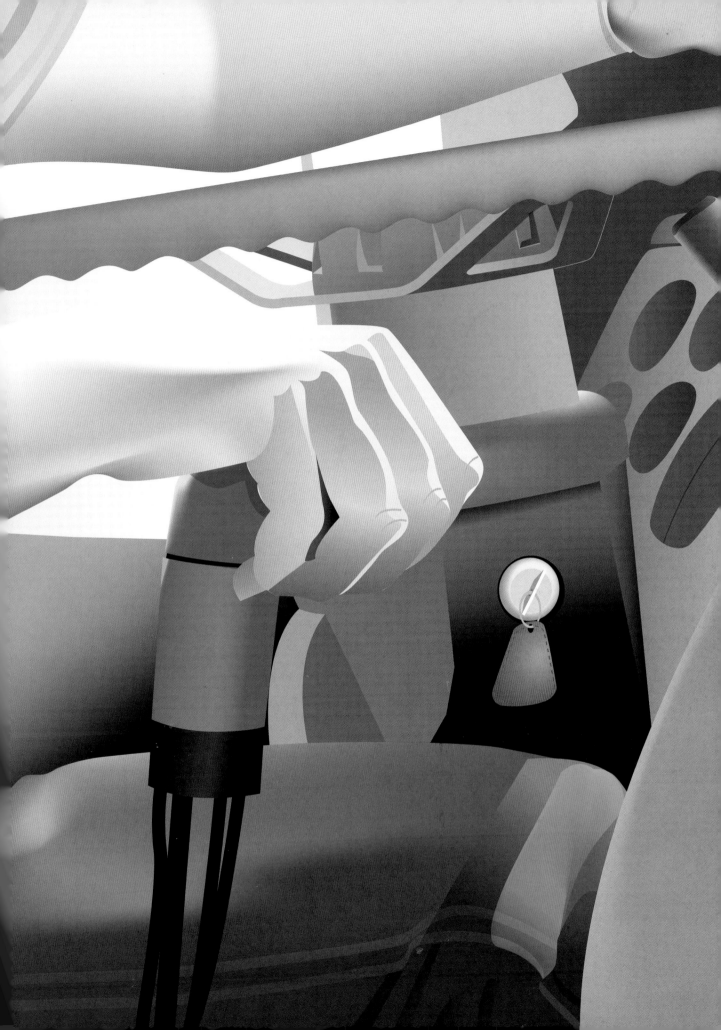

and watches out for others.

He's on the move

but always says hello.

When traffic is slow,

Daddy stops

and grabs a bite.

Daddy's on time

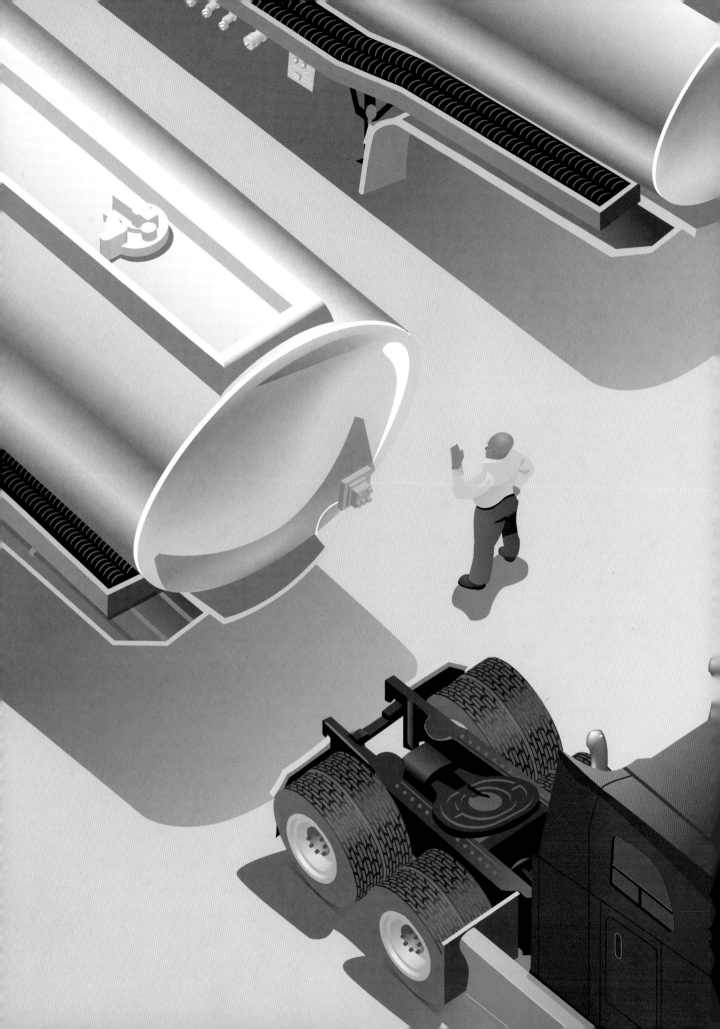

because
there is
more
work
to do.

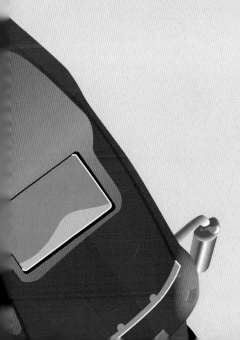

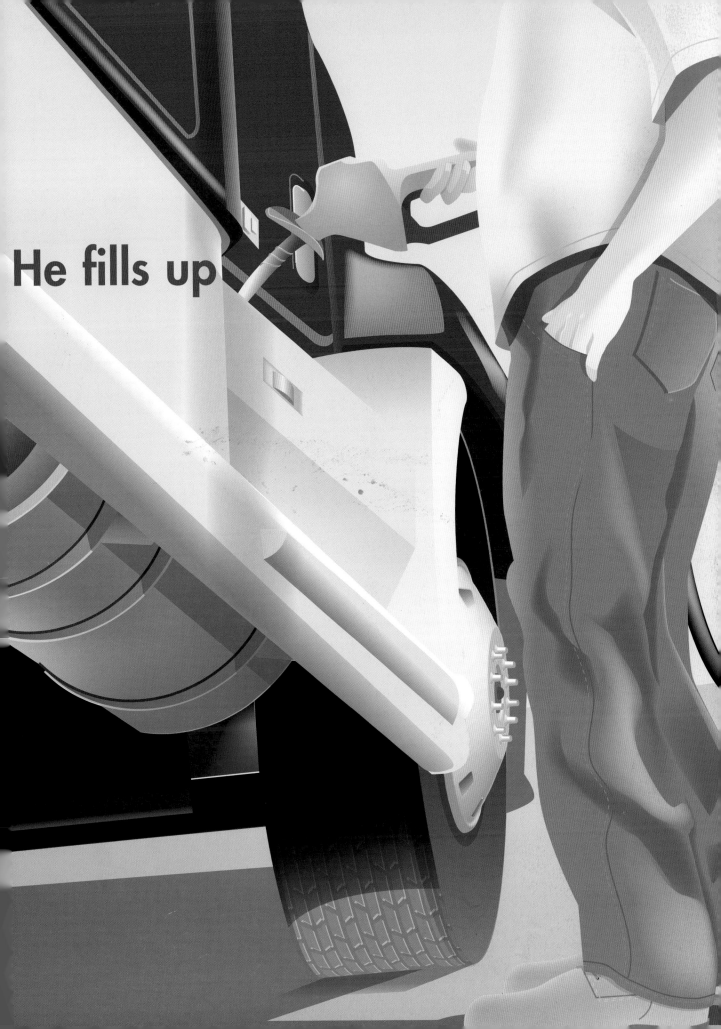

He fills up

and drives